THE LITTLE BOOK OF 99 DAILY POSITIVE AFFIRMATIONS

Be Uplifted Everday!

Heba Hamzeh

CONTENTS

ABOUT THE AUTHOR

Heba Hamzeh is a mother to three who inspired her vocation as an author and has published three fiction books:

Prince Zaaki And The Royal Sword of Luella
Prince Zaaki And The Momentous Battle of The Kingdoms
Prince Zaaki And The Knights of The Altar of Truth

Dear Reader,

I hope that this book full of affirmations helps you gain confidence and belief in yourself . These affirmations have helped me immensely as well as aiding my children. I always share affirmations with loved ones to motivate and encourage them, especially when they are in need of positivity. These affirmations will help lead you to where you want to go in life. Happy reading!

Heba

READ THE AFFIRMATIONS AND SAY THEM OUT LOUD.

Say positive affirmations out loud so your mind and body can hear you.

Believe the positive affirmations you are saying.

Repeat the positive affirmations 3 times a day so your mind and body start to believe them.

Work towards your goals and never give up.

Strive to be the best version of yourself.

Believe in yourself.

LET THE WORDS RESONATE
WITHIN YOUR BODY AND MIND.
BELIEVE THE WORDS.
LET POSITIVITY INTO
YOUR MIND.
RELEASE ALL THE NEGATIVITY.

POSITIVE AFFIRMATIONS

You are amazing
You are wonderful
You are great
You will achieve everything you set your mind to
You have the power to succeed in your life
You deserve love
You deserve greatness
You deserve happiness

DAILY AFFIRMATIONS

I am loved
I am calm
I am healthy
I am happy
I am successful
I am blessed

My life is full of love
My life is full of calmness
My life is full of happiness
My life is full of success
My life is a blessing

I am exuding love
I am exuding kindness
I am exuding compassion
I am exuding fortitude
I am exuding calmness
I am exuding success
I am exuding health
I am blessed

Opportunity surrounds me
Abundance surrounds me
Health surrounds me
Love surrounds me
Kindness surrounds me

POSITIVE THOUGHTS

I am successful
I am happy
I am calm
I am healthy
My mind is healthy
My body is healthy

HEALTH

My body is healing everyday
And with every minute of every day
I am healing and getting better
My body is healing
My mind is healing
I am in control of my health
I am healthy
I am full of energy
I am great

STRESSFUL SITUATIONS

I am at peace
Peace surrounds me
My mind is peaceful
My mind is calm
My mind is rational
I am in control of my mind

STUDY AND WORK

I am absorbing all the information in front of me
I am learning efficiently
I am achieving my desired goals
I have achieved my desired goals
I am capable of this and more

HAPPINESS

I am loved
I love
I am cared for
I care for others
I am appreciated
I appreciate others
I am happy
I spread my happiness
I am blessed
I spread my blessings

LET GO OF NEGATIVITY

I choose to release my negativity
I choose to be positive
My mind is full of positivity
My body is healthy

BE KIND

Be kind to yourself
Be kind to your body
Be kind to your mind
Be kind to your soul
Be kind to your heart

I am kind to myself
I am kind to my body
I am kind to my mind
I am kind to my soul
I am kind you my heart

I release all negativity
I accept all positivity
My hands are open to positivity

I am worthy of love
I am worthy of respect
I am worthy of health
I am worthy of success
I am worthy of opportunity
I am worthy of greatness

BE OPEN TO

My heart is open to love
My mind is open to knowledge
My body is open to health
My life is open to opportunity
My hands are open to wealth
I am open to success
I am open to boundless achievements

HOW TO LIVE
EVERYDAY

GO OUT EVERYDAY WITH A
SMILE ON YOUR FACE

SPREAD KINDNESS
AND KINDNESS SHALL
RETURN TO YOU

SPREAD LOVE
AND LOVE SHALL RETURN TO YOU

SPREAD JOY
AND JOY SHALL RETURN TO YOU

SPREAD HAPPINESS
AND HAPPINESS SHALL
RETURN TO YOU

WANT IT

DESIRE IT

VISUALISE IT

BELIEVE IT

SEE IT HAS ALREADY HAPPENED

ACHIEVE IT

APPRECIATE IT

YOU DESERVE IT!

WRITE 3 AFFIRMATIONS

Now it is your turn to write down three positive affirmations for you (try not to have any negative words in there for example, 'not' is a negative word):

Say out loud and repeat your positive affirmations three times a day.

Printed in Great Britain
by Amazon